Cutting tl

Katy V

First published in 2018
by Hesterglock
Bristol
www.hesterglockpress.weebly.com

These poems are a work of fiction. Some names, characters
and incidents portrayed in it are the work of the author's
imagination. Any resemblance to actual persons, living or
dead, events or locales is entirely coincidental.

All poems copyright © 2018 Katy Wareham Morris
Cover Design: Paul Hawkins/Katy Wareham Morris

ISBN-13: 978-1999915346
ISBN-10: 1999915348

For chicks, especially Barbara . . .

Acknowledgements

I am incredibly grateful to Paul Hawkins and Sarer Scotthorne at Hesterglock for giving me the opportunity to publish these sometimes risky and sometimes difficult poems. I really appreciate their support and encouragement, which has led me to believe that I am, and can be a poet.

Thanks also to Dr Lynn Parr who first published *At the Widows' Clumps* in *The Curlew* earlier this year.

My thanks to everyone who has inspired me in writing this book, particularly all of the women who I am lucky to have in my life, but especially Ruth Stacey who has been my musick.

I must thank my parents for enabling me to become a loud and passionate woman, who is not afraid of her body nor her sexuality. I hope to be able to guide my children as well as they have guided me. I thank my brother for being my best friend.

Finally, I must thank my husband, Simon for continuing to work with me through what is a testing life, and for helping me to bring two magnificent little people into this beautiful, yet broken world; I had never been so inspired until I had my babies.

Contents

From the Never-Heard Bird

La Lune   Erato   Eve   Loba

Am I now the Priestess,
as you have given me the rites,
the power to bear (to be)?
To become the new cornucopia
and embrace this discord.
I have shared so many times before
but never had the faith.

Am I now to be worshipped
and adored, as you have been before me?
Have you touched me with your light
and passed on the permission to write?

You, who bear no truth and refuse
to answer. You, whom I love
yet who cannot love in return.
Is it good for you?
Reply if like,
without shouting, gently this time,
in the new serenity I have created:
my Voice is without volume.

I shall speak through this love,
and you shall not be damned
nor condemned in the moonlight,
not dragged up, held up, shut up.

I surge forth -
You shall bear this fruit.

On your Becoming

White dawn says goodbye to surrender,
binding vitality in a permanent cloak.
Sorcery claims bleeding is hypnosis:
half-hatched genesis.

Hoarse and calling: words falling
        continue blinking.

Metal being: hairs listening
        continue breathing.

Stewing

China tea cups tinkled all around,
but

we were ignorant.   I couldn't give a
You were drinking hot Earl Grey,
I sipped my orange Assam.   I slurped my orange Assam
                                                    loudly and through teeth.

My butter-soaked crumpet had just arrived
when you lowered your paper,
looked me in the eye
and smiled shrewdly -
I knew you were remembering

I licked my lips gently,   when I fucked you hard,
savouring the taste.   licked my lips and
                                                    savoured the taste.

From Wifey

No longer in command, but still cooking
sweet Pinky, your favourite brownie;
drinking your coffee, and hearing the
sound of your velvet purity

without peer, a rose was a rose, and
this war is worse than any war.

This dainty birdie is made weaker
without cutting your close-cropped hair,
and catching sight of your brooch

gone so long, Lovey, and
loving more and more.

Your Boss could not stop them taking
your children, and since, our dog has
stopped barking. We long for your
questions; your notes in the morning

Strong-strong husband,

the bell hasn't stopped ringing,
but whilst you're sleeping mr,
this Baby Bright has stopped twinkling.

Baby precious boy
baby precious sleep.

Homeward Bound

It was late and she had no money left.
    A childish mistake.
Her friends didn't want to leave, but she knew she was
wasted, she knew she had to go. Plus she had no money left.
She was only at the pub down the road, so if she left now it
wouldn't be too too late
    to be walking
down the street she grew up on, phone in one hand,
keys in the other.

She headed towards the bus shelter and as she
passed the broken glass (local yobs at it again),
    she saw someone not too far in the distance –
    a recognisable shape.
    Who else wore a parka in the summer heat?
She called out to her pal from school. He stopped and turned,
    then smiled.
She jogged to catch him up and realised
just how warm it was. He must have been sweating
under there. He'd lived two doors down all her life.

Five minutes later, after some small talk about the
summer, the night at the pub and some old school
memories, they laughed about his parka. She hadn't
looked closely at his smile before –
    lots of teeth.
She was reminded of a cartoon crocodile, and then

at the top of the entryway that lead to the back
of Mrs. Harris' house. She'd never been so close
to the oily blue bricks that paved the floor. She'd never
noticed how unevenly they'd been laid or
how the poppies were scattered in various cracks, corners and
edges. Now,
    she saw it all -

the poppies were
burnt orange-red like the sweat-drenched
lining of the parka.
Even in the dark she could see their colour,

feel their heat.

She came out of the entryway

                             and

waited.
      He followed,
doing up his parka. She saw one small pearl of sweat
by his nose. He was talking about the summer,
the pub and old school memories. They walked
down the road towards the chippy.
      She wasn't sure if summer had a smell.
He stopped to get a cone,
      she carried on home.

She wondered whether the parka made him do it.

'Around 90% of rapes are committed by known men, and often by someone who the survivor has previously trusted or loved'. Rapecrisis.

Pills / Pillow Talk

i spend a lot of time in the dark just
listening it breathes all on its own
the rhythm has the pace of waiting
pressing like a heavy blanket thick
and silky that swallows i reach out
to grab it but it falls through my fin
gers and then I am waving it is not
a well coming friend still the reflect
ion is disquieting familiar glossy an
d lulling me into mystery i am loos
ing limbs and my head to nothing
everything is something missing i
ts shape, its meaning tumbling into
bottomless lochs that were walls th
under clouds threaten to whip me in
to a storm i notice i am alone then i
switch on the light i

From Courtney

He needed me like I needed the red lipstick; it was my thing, it still is my thing. He is still my thing; I'm forever his wife, his queen. They called it strange love, but what's strange about a guy and girl so hooked on fucking falling for each other. It helped that he needed me for something, something else. I knew it then but he didn't notice my dresses didn't quite fit, so I gave him the black tar to coat his heart until I could explain the fit. He knew I had tits and zits – a sincere enough nineties reason for living. I'm always late for everything. He waited. Time flies by when you're high, even if your mind plays slow. Nothing is an accident. Would he wake up? We loved each other and that's all that matters. We sucked each others' scars and then the tar lay thick to fill the ridges. We were both vampires, I guess he got everlasting life. For everyone else, being a bitch gave them a boner. He believed the tea dresses and didn't notice the tears. I wanted us to do all the shows. We never got to do the live on-stage sex thing; I couldn't find a baby doll dirty enough, or with a big enough bow. He got tired too. There were doll parts everywhere, inside and out. He was still my best friend. I asked and he answered. He always answered. I always tried to impress him. I copped some dope one night and after that for the next few months. Alcohol just didn't sit right with him. We wanted our baby. We needed new friends. I got him to wear boxers, he was such a tacky thing. Everyone stole everything from me: dresses, lyrics, riffs, guitars, shoes. Madonna stole my eyeliner. People dream of killing me. I'm not a model, I'm credible. Who knew when it would fuck up, but it did. You must've been psychic or something. Sorry, not sorry.

Biology / Reflections

You've a body
that responds to instinct:
immediate impulse,

that writhes when touched.
Never apologise -
when you want it
for your own
energy.

Be robust in your desire,
find it -

it is not a flower.
You decide when to

At Coco Beach

I am night

Moon's arms stroking
my haunches,
pulling my bristles.

Waxy knot
confusing thick silk.

Bedding down on gallet blanket

tusks flinch and I smell
paper shells, torn
fraying history.

Hooves hover,
crags cry grey, salty murder.

Moon's arms pinching
my ribs,
pulling my tail.

Inhaling anticipation

Shed new sores,
wounds weep

Jaw gapes...

Stars in my eyes

From Norma Jeane

I am supposed to be seducing,
but instead wondering -
consumed by the shimmying sway.
Forcing the feeling of fullness,
moving closer to your back, your neck.

My hands mirror my curves –
created for me, I have learnt
to flaunt them. They dance
like my hips,
ribboning your back, your neck.

My dress is too pure for keeping,
white nylon, charged.
I desire cotton but jewelled costume
is more appealing:
pool-lighting my back, my neck, those hips.

I glance at my reflection in your wanting,
your face recognises my image
but I am struggling.

Postcard

Front
The rhododendrons and azaleas are out of this world,
no really, they're almost alien, they're huge, and
the sound of the bees is mesmerising – they say hello.
Today, I chased a butterfly down the path, later I'll go
wandering in the rain, and tomorrow I'll sit in my
simple room and not think about you. There is no
peace here: nature is noisy, their symphony distracting –
it's no holiday. If I have a moment, I might brave
the chattering night to call, but it gets thick dark and
I'm not sure you'd see the point. It would be difficult
for you to see the beauty. This is beauty, here.

Back
Someone told me the name of the plants and flowers
to impress you but I don't know why I thought I should
impress you. It isn't charming to think of anthropomorphised
flora politely greeting you when we can barely breathe
next to each other. I want to live in the moment, but my
brain is wracked by our feuding and fucking. I think
about them endlessly and then cry furiously and then
finger myself until I'm screaming your name for wholly
different reasons. There is no peace. I long to call you
so you could hear my post-come breathing and you'd
get hard, and it would be beautiful.

Spring Triptych

I

I'm singing whilst crying,
learning and choking.
I'm passionate and rageful,
lustful and hopeful,
barely regrettable.
I'm hunting and humming
Who put these glasses on?

Watching near-sighted
time laid brick by brick,
every click into place.

II

It's a shame you couldn't
love the same, the way I had.
High hopes and expectations,

putting more into you.
Everything ended up on me.

I simplified you,
gave energy to reason.
Now, I've got none.
Thank you for my children.

III

I knew something was coming: the room went dusty and grey,
hail came down on the flat roof and you said you couldn't
hear me. I lifted the glasses off my eyes and rested the bridge
on my forehead, it dug a little; I pressed and it felt good. I
didn't know whether the hammering was in my head so I
closed my eyes and opened them to test: my vision was still
blurred and you were still talking.

From Ziggy

I'm a soaring superqueer.
Be happy and meet me,
keep your radio playing
as I descend from space.
Come
to greet your omnisexual prophet,

let them blow your mind,
your lover, your neighbour
sparkles.
Let your cosmic soul
play it hazy, play it low

and fill those big, thick
alien boogie boots.
I'm with you and
any secret crush,
wild love and raw

power tears you from the inside,
pulls it all apart when I
Enter
one awesome star.

The lady starman changes
clothes and sheds skin.
A sometimes fatal femme
daydreaming messages
in the sky, in your
groin.

Are you scared of forever?

This Time

I

Enchant me again
with your sweet melodious mood
        sing me the song of the Nightingale -

Are you singing every time you

Grow your apples in the garden
give us one or two or three
        never stop this Autoeroticism -

Let me go stroke after stroke

Purse your bounteous Bird-like lips
your invisible silk in season
        a sweet kiss

Glorious Fruit! Plentiful Harvest!

Fearlessly feed me your Apple Blossom
the fruits of our labour
        making tender musick -

Howling, wet and misty Loba sings

See us in the distance
casting shadows
        hear me roar

II

Was this a mistake? Errors in perception
        blurring whurring whizzing
Mind buzzing

She creeps slowly
        biting bleeding hungering yearning
Fragile and needy

Eve offers fruit wine
Where is her mind?
        playing with Thumper

Daggers of light cast shadows on her
slender physique made tort / taut
made agile
        made clean

Softly you weep
        I whimper with desire
my medicine my punishment
        your envy your charm

Your love for this Bird
believe that I can hold you
a tender caress a sweet kiss
        let me go

Let me hang your coat
        bathe in my insatiable desire
luscious red you be
        Come

Dance again and never stop
hear this Bird
        make Musick

III

Come to me in the night
when I am
distracted by other talk

Jump on me and strip me -
    I shall sing an unsung song

Karaoke Sing Song / Testament of Love
for Diane Di Prima

heavy beats   punching pounding
     throbbing in my chest underneath my breast
beating vessel chamber of desire
electricity through my chambers
surge   forge forth   heat
            Beat
a red door of lust for you

I read your magick words losing myself
both inside and out I am feeling you
want to keep you inside
     hoping to magickally evoke you

picking you ticking tickling tinkering
     tingling   ting ting ting
                  Zing

puppet tup it tip it up pick it up
               murmuring
twinge   pull string
       (stroke after stroke)
linger no longer
     myself left in the music of you

pip in my mouth sour grape

the female is ductile and so is this one

drip drip sip my blood
        (as water I am pouring)
I am brimming filling and feeling full too
getting wide with a child I did not bear
vessel   channel   chalice full

neck next
      mount   mouth of you

your rhythm is my stillness
to wear your dried ink and perform
I am the never-heard bird

ting ting ting
        Zing sing
               (applause?)

From Peaches

This song leapt from my vulva,
fell straight in your mouth;
you salivate, scream for another -
fuck this.

You kiss the next one,
it spreads - another dick
hard, my lips done.

Take a dick in every hole,
that's what you told me to do.
Now I'm telling you -
fuck this.

It's thick, it's hard,
I'm wearing it, but you
still see my clit. Take his
too, hard flesh in your ass
will make the biggest hit.

I'm singing for my girls' pussies,
for their titties, clitties and come.
My vulva pants, tells you -
take more dicks.
Fuck this.

Let me and him and them
come on your face.

We shall come. Fuck this.

Pillow Fight

Marking your territory, you crawl
inside and burrow –
        burying your dirty bone.

Gnawing at the sinuous thicket
that has grown too long without you;
        thorny pleasure pricks your lips.

You are not deterred by the taste,
yet your snarling and licking
        will not destroy this bush.

This rampage ravages me whole,
I am forced to return the favour:
        meagre petals thrash your gong.

You wallow in the mud and I am
feeling full as I eat you –
        my desire bleeding.

Your scent will no longer linger
but stain. I am listening,
        whimpering...

Dinner Date

For Sappho

I seem to be desire
waiting before you; but
     I am the Priestess /
Poetess who confronts you:
     my tortured voice screams.

Emerging from the chrysalis
     to match my will,
you are enchanted.
     My hideous laugh bubbles
beneath the breast.

Tending the flames
beneath your skin,
     my tongue flicks:
     I breathe fire.

My eyes see your fear,
your ears burn now:
     my truth makes you quiver.

You are exposed,
shivering with sweat;
     I am deep beneath you.

The grass sways violently,
you are close to death;

     words dissolve unheard
     the other goddess is green

From Naomi

He sits at the table and reads the menu: hunks of meat,
stripped lean and fleshed out with fillers,
chunked into tender pieces. His mouth waters.
Grabbing the waitress's pussy, he makes his order:
'No disgusting animals here'.

He sits at the table and jokes about dating his daughter
and photo-shaming his flabby assistant. She
went on another diet and lost a few pounds this month,
she kept her job. They're celebrating.
She made it; she's a beautiful piece of ass.

He sits at the table and they're about ready to talk
about the punishments, the punishments for abortions.
Then he notices the waitress's pancake tits,
he knows a great surgeon, he can pay for it.
They all co-sign.

Best Actor

Will you put your arm around the knight,
caress its back and stroke the reel's
five spokes? Each strong rib makes
you smile, gives you shivers.
Will you let your rank alco-breath
mist it's shiny face, which you cannot
see because you hold it so close
your eyes are blurred, as you polish
its long sword with your eager fingers?
Will you let it lie between your fleshy
man's legs and tuck its head underneath
the bottom of your t-shirt?
Will you show it your dick?
Would you press it against
someone else and ask them
to lick it, suck it, fuck it?
Would you be angry if the knight
suddenly spoke and said, 'You cow,
I've had better sex than this'?

Freud

The door was locked with a pale green ribbon

meaning the grass is –
    on the other side
and the monster's eyes
    the envy of it all.

Meaning bought new with cash:
peace on earth, the world –
    one opened, as another
    trapped in space.

Meaning safety and security,
    hero's passage
into the bowels of –
enduring harvest of sick slime.

Meaning a fresh start,
lambs and spring and
    one that grows inside:
brimming cup.

Meaning it can be healed:
    universal comfort,
blessed at the altar

    green is free to go.

Becoming

I faced the future as a block of heat:
a sack of stoneless cherries on fire.
Burning and heavy, growing already,
I was the rite to be. I was energy.

I was not at peace and I did not bring it with me.
Pounding and kicking in the un-still air
no one dared soothe me. Ready for action,

I was sucked into time by a squall,
rocking on my shell, uneasy.
Made wild by the gusty sway,

I was impatient, intolerable and grouchy.
I was not really knowing.

I was not smooth and silky.
I was sticky.
I was ugly.

From Cis Woman

I try to see it in your eyes,
any trace in your body.
Is it wrong to feel deceived?
You lean in to tell me your truth
and I flinch, the image seeded,
growing with the others,
planting doubt, and fear,
resentment, anger.
I've worked so hard to thin the forest,
don't tell me how to walk
or what trees need thinning.
You are a new fruit,
sometimes prickly.

Wishful Thinking

Looking back, I was brave. I was lucky. He was
      kind and kept checking. Maybe because he was older.
I can watch it now, watch the memory play back like a bad
episode of *Hollyoaks* – the late night version. All bad acting.
Something left on the cutting room floor.

It surprises me that I wanted it. It surprises me that I knew I
wanted it. I said clearly: 'I want it'. Ballsy. He was
      already on top of me. Jimi was there too, he watched us.
His eyes shiny black and his face like November – all shades of
smoke and fire. The naked girl lolled on his hanging acoustic,
right above my head. In the 90s, he was
      all long hair and under-cuts and Nirvana and guitars
whilst I was a Spice Girl. I stared at the stretched out limbs of
the painted girl and the black dapple-effect wallpaper. I'd
never seen anything like it. I'd never felt anything like

the fibrous coral-coloured blanket that hid under the fluro-
striped duvet; it had its own sound. A duvet, a blanket, a
sheet –
      all that weight. He had a drawer full of condoms, just
waiting

Knotted scarves tied together in a rope threaded inside. Each
big knot jammed. Slow, even threading didn't stop. It didn't
hurt. There was no tear, no rip, no release. Intuition told me it
was about to be over. I gripped his back like I'd seen on a bad
episode of *Hollyoaks* – the late night version. All bad acting.
Something left on the cutting room floor.

After, I was pleased - I hadn't been scared and I hadn't been
hurt. I don't think I felt a thing. Why would people do it
again? The whole world lives off it. I'd have to do it again

I went to the mirrored bathroom, wiped away a little smear
the colour of flamingoes,
and I was pleased. Pleased it was easy
and polite.

Romanticism

I love my eyelashes when I
                    c
                      r
                        y
because I'm   back

                                                              to
the future   and thinking it's working believing that all the
false
starts were worth it and we're finally t i c k i n g   **over**

The darkness

        of our time together resurfaces during an exchange
about vans and prams
the clenched fist that is your tone and the needle-point
                        s
                      p
                        i
                          t from your t o n g u e

Sqeeeeeeeze my lips tight and feel the   Beat
my foolish heart had

Slow Motion / Overwinter

I find myself wishing your life away into your next phase
making things easier on me cajoling myself with thoughts of a
settled more happy you nightdreaming about a contented
babe you satisfied and restful my beguiling falsehood it's for
me to make your life your little being easier on me who
already has the world

All that winter the flight of butterflies was soft.
They scarcely survive in the cold, but wings tapped
on distant train tracks reminding me they were
near and still

You are happy just blissful happy next to my milky skin your
eyes smile I am yours no longer mystery remembering you
were part of me

tap-drip flap-flying through sleepy nights.
One occupied a nest: quick inside a coral shell,
cushioned not on the beach but on my shelf.

We are one body again I am forgiven soon you will stir and so
will your sister

It appeared just when you thought it was gone.
Chasing the smell of the summer stretch.

From Roop
Sati Mata

The bhopas told Pabuji's story many times,
now it is me standing at the gate:
not able to change that lengha
you thought pretty; not able to make the roti.
Not even Princess Mira Bai's
words of bhakti comfort me.

My pain is never to be a mother:
half-alive, expecting nothing.
Not able to live like Sandili;
there are no more leftovers, Pati.

I long to make the sacrifice.
My dharma; my Stridharma.
You will reach salvation:
our families free from reincarnation.

Launching myself boldly onto your pyre,
as one offering to the Gods:

I am dignified
I am pure
I am sati

No longer hoping you are oak,
me lime; you vine;
me red rose bush.

In our smoke
We fuse
We entwine

Sorry for Watching Benefit Porn

Food bank, then doctor
     to see your child smile again.
Your faceless eyes stone.

Your token won't work
     today, you are not enough.
No smiling this week.

Therapy

Week one: Is this...
carefully knitted together? We curl up (hide) beside thick
pillows of polite, romantic fabric, seducing

my skin was itchy, scratchy, rashy

Week two: Is this...
the doll I kept? Conjuring my (buried) childhood reveries
about mummies and daddies

the baby that came is

Week three: Is this...
covering a nasty beneath? The hot, sticky mess
that wept, ached to be touched and spread between us

My face says it all

Week four: Is this...
turf ours? Our piece of the world that is sinking

I start reaching for

Week five: Is this...
passing? The split shreds further when people start asking (if
we're still thinking of divorce)

Every Thursday

A tired, withered smile,
she peers from a shrinking doorway.
Recognising but not quite knowing,
smiling anyway. Tighter permy curls.

Inside her house I see the heat
but she's struggling with the fire again.

Have you been out this week?

'He's working in a school'.
Finding money.

Overwhelmed, your birthday cards confuse you.

'Mother was a worker'.
'Mother was kinder'.
'Mother was dead'.

From Hilda

Wild iris dancing
in vicious sea,
whipping waves swallow
mystic twin in foam -
Stolen.

Petals dissolved in salt spray -
abandoned.
Roses thrive
in coarse sand,
rooted, watching.

Birthday

Before

Thank you for the four tender kisses
you gave me before bed,
as if you knew and
wanted to surprise me early.

In recent years I have become glum about
a catalogue of un-thumbed books and blank pads.
It's tough when no one gives a fuck.
You must've known
I was a slowly deflating balloon.

After

Today I bathed in a sea of petals:
soft warm water kissed the very rim,
almost sinking into the scented
wet affection of ylang ylang.

stroke after stroke

I sat up to distract from temptation -
Buddha-like in the bath
I closed my eyes to restore peace,
but my teeth scratched.

too deep to take pain away

Something drained away,
whilst the flames licked.

the sea burned

At the Widows' Clumps

We plant trees in a place only they know.
Silver needles grow dense and fierce,
healing the craters, filling the clearing.
They grow too fast.

Nurtured by the lush soil,
alpine aromas are their presence in the air.

Persistent in this hand-to-hand combat:
waiting for the wolves to come home.

Adrift, wearing white and writing:
waiting for your strong arm,
your uncanny hand.

From Laura

Dear JT,
You came when I needed you. You weren't my child,but you
saved the one I had from being motherless. You were the kid
that I couldn't escape, and I really needed to find peace for
you. Your life wasn't a dream. It wasn't commercial potential.
Wasn't it funny when everyone started wearing the penis
bones?

Dear Savannah,
You made this real. I gave it to you. You never wanted it to
end, but you wanted to come out. You couldn't be a celebrity.
I still can't believe they thought your tits and pussy were man-
made. You were my aura.

Dear Speedie,
I know you were ridiculous, but that meant no one came
looking for me. I had someone to be, someone who was
needed. Even I wasn't expecting the lie. You gave me a
theatre. You were a kid too.

Dear Geoff,
You got to be in a band, like you wanted. Your jealousy made
us all human again. Now you can write your own book and
enjoy being Vice President of that. I always said you should be
a rock star.

Dear Astor,
Everyone thought we were the jailers.

Dear Emily,
You were the social worker I knew I needed. The one that
never found me. You found JT and that was good enough. It's
a shame people thought you were a star-fucking vampire
Fagin.

They were all of me; the pages attached themselves to flesh.
With love, us all.

Reprise / Vermiculture Porno

boom   boom click clit
boom   boom click clit

and so it begins
ear worms grow
put your back into it

we fly in the night
straight into your ear
your mouth, your ass
we ride

bitch   bitch butch hoe
slag   slag slag hag
boom   boom click clit
boom   boom click clit

can we talk about vulvas?
my clit, my lips, my discharge,
my menstrual blood?
We did -
it   it   it   it   willlllllll
                              come
whorrrrrre slut
angelprincessvirgin
slut
whorrrrrre slut
angelprincessvirgin
slut

by any other name
mystic mythic manic
                      mute
boom boom click clit
boom boom click clit
cute sassy sexy slinky
fiesty funny
          fucked
hot trashy tasty tacky
frigid fanny

choked

invisible worms
thread their ribbons
tie you in silk
bind you in green
your ankles burn
you're bleeding
                    crimson joy

motherwifeteacher
lover
motherwifeteacher
shudddddder
boom boom click clit
boom boom click clit

pussy kitten catty
                    skank
foxy floozy nasty
                    vamp
boom boom click clit
boom boom click clit
your harmony made me weep
discordant dissonance
                    (dark secret love)
you told me was sweet
your symphony   stuck
deep throat incongruity
gag gag
  gagggggging

spit spit spit
(sometimes I like it)

this musick charms
thick fleshy worms
that fly in the night
tickle my clit, my nipples

your ear, your ass
not so safe in your bed
                    (destroy?)

boom boom click clit
boom boom click clit
bolshy bossy bubbly
                bitch
coochie coochie
                cunt

this worm will thread your snatch
not such a ghastly gash

irrational mating shhhrrrrilllll
to call the worms from twat
(what a bombshell?)
these Birds love worms

thanks for the airhead in my bed
luscious lips lascivious licks
sassy worm-like dicks

boom boom click clit
boom boom click clit
this rose is not sick

Author Notes

From Wifey
This poem is written from the perspective of Alice B. Toklas, the life partner of Gertrude Stein. Toklas and Stein would leave each other notes and love letters, and this poem has borrowed fragments from these, as well as from Stein's 1913 poem, *Sacred Emily*, lines of which were heavily promoted by Toklas.

From Courtney
This is a found poem from the perspective of Courtney Love, based on an article published in the September 1992 issue of *Vanity Fair* written by Lynn Hirschberg.

From Norma Jeane
This poem is written from the perspective of the icon we know as Marilyn Monroe, born Norma Jeane Mortenson.

From Ziggy
This poem is written from the perspective of David Bowie's alter-ego, Ziggy Stardust and is informed by the lyrics on the 1972 concept album, *The Rise and Fall of Ziggy Stardust and the Spiders from Mars*.

From Peaches
This poem is written from the perspective of the electronic musician and performance artist, Peaches, born Merrill Beth Nisker.

From Naomi
This poem is written from the perspective of Naomi Klein who is a recognised international, political speaker. This poem also uses fragments from Donald Trump's interviews and TV appearances.

From Roop
This poem is written from the perspective of Roop Kanwar, who was hailed as a *Sati Mata*. At the time of her death she was 18 years old and had been married for 8 months; there were conflicting news reports about whether her death was voluntary.

From Hilda
This poem is written from the perspective of Hilda Doolittle,
known as HD, who was influenced by her two great loves,
Ezra Pound and Frances Josepha Gregg. Doolittle experienced
relationships with both, who then also had a relationship with
each other.

From Laura
This poem is written from the perspective of Laura Albert
after watching the 2016 documentary, *Author: The JT LeRoy
Story* directed by Jeff Feuerzeig.

About the author

Katy Wareham Morris is a writer and lecturer in media and culture. She is particularly interested in identity politics and digital humanities. Her debut pamphlet, *Inheritance* was a poetry duet with Ruth Stacey, and was published by Mother's Milk Press in 2017. Her poems have also featured in webzines including *I am not a silent poet* and *Ink, Sweat and Tears*. She was a founding member of the Women's Equality Party and created the Birmingham branch. This is her first full collection of poetry. She lives in Stourbridge, West Midlands with her family. You can follow Katy on Twitter @katy_wm, or find her website at katywarehammorris.com

42910181R00029

Printed in Poland
by Amazon Fulfillment
Poland Sp. z o.o., Wrocław